By the same author:

Canadian One Act Plays for Women

Our Own Particular JANE

by

Joan Mason Hurley

A ROOM OF ONE'S OWN
PRESS

BOX 5215, STATION B   VICTORIA, B.C.

ISBN 0-919998-00-3

First Printing: November, 1975.

Cover Design by James Bennett

Printing by Idealetter Services Ltd.,
Victoria, B.C.

to

Freydis

for many
reasons

Preface

In each succeeding generation members of my family have written about our famous ancestor, Jane Austen. In the beginning there was my great grandfather, James Edward Austen-Leigh. He wrote the very first book ever published about his aunt, the Memoir of Jane Austen, 1870. This was followed by Life and Letters of Jane Austen, 1913, a collaboration by James Edward's son and grandson, William and R. A. Austen-Leigh. Other, lesser works have included Personal Aspects of Jane Austen, 1920, by Mary Austen-Leigh, and Jane Austen and Steventon, 1939, by Emma Austen-Leigh, daughter and granddaughter of James Edward.

It was therefore with some trepidation and with the weight of generations looking over my shoulder, that I, great great granddaughter of Jane's eldest brother, the Rev. James Austen, approached the task of writing a play about Jane Austen.

In the first place it could not, by definition, be a 'play' in the regular meaning of the word, because no Janeite would countenance words being put into the mouths of Jane's characters. Besides, I, myself, would not wish to perpetrate anything so unseemly. I, therefore, decided my play would have to be a 'piece of theatre'; But it was not to consist of a hodge podge of the best-known scenes thrown together without theme or reason beyond the arbitrary choice of the compiler. This would not satisfy me, nor, I felt, would it sustain an audience. There must be some linear development, and the logical solution was to tell the story of Jane's life, illustrated by her own letters, scenes and characters. The only liberty I allowed myself was a little reluctant pruning. For what is perfection on the printed page occasionally becomes a little lengthy for the more impatient, dramatic ear of a live audience. The result, I hoped, would be acceptable both to addicts as well as to those who were lucky enough to be discovering Jane Austen for the first time.

J. M. H.

Victoria, B. C.   (nee Joan Austen-Leigh)

NOTE

In the process of devising this script, I have been greatly helped by Anthony Jenkins, head of Honours English, University of Victoria, and Patricia Wainman Wood of the Department of Theatre. As actors they have assisted me by reading aloud the first drafts of the manuscript and as critics they have given me the benefit of informed and cultivated opinion. To them, and to Evanne Murray who has lightened my labours by her skill at the typewriter, my warmest thanks.

To those of our audience whose favourite
characters are omitted, we offer our
apologies. Mr. Woodhouse, in particular,
sends his regrets. But since his feelings
are well known, he declines to add to the
length of the evening by his presence for
'the sooner every party breaks up the better'

<u>Our Own Particular Jane</u> was first performed at the Phoenix Theatre, University of Victoria, for the Jane Austen Bicentenary Commemoration on April 3, 1975. The play was directed by Maurice Harty with the following cast:

      Jane .... Trish Grainge

      Narrator .... Reg Terry

      Mrs. Bennet, Miss Bates, etc........ Patricia Wainman-Wood

      Edward Austen, Sir Walter Elliot, etc.. Anthony Jenkins

On April 7, the play was broadcast over the Canadian Broadcasting Corporation F.M. network, directed by Robert Chesterman.

To the Director:

<u>Our Own Particular Jane</u> may be performed by either four or six actors. The division of parts is left to the director's discretion. If only four people are used, however, it is suitable if the actress who plays Jane, plays also the sympathetic parts of Elizabeth Bennet, Anne Elliot and Catherine Morland.

Act 1

JANE: "It is a truth universally acknowledged that a single man in possession of a good fortune must be in want of a wife."

NARRATOR: This, most famous of all opening sentences, was composed by a girl of twenty, in an obscure country parsonage, nearly two hundred years ago. Yet Jane Austen was to become a middle-aged woman before Pride and Prejudice ever appeared in print. Published anonymously in her lifetime, after her death her works were virtually unknown and barely appreciated. That is, until about the middle of the nineteenth century, then it was that stray visitors began increasingly to invade Winchester Cathedral. They wanted to see Miss Austen's grave. This puzzled the verger, and he made inquiries.

VERGER· (An uneducated voice) "Can you tell me, was there something particular about that lady?"

NARRATOR: Something particular indeed. Macauley placed her next to Shakespeare and declared:

MACAULEY: (Pompous) "She is a woman of whom England is justly proud."

NARRATOR: Charlotte Bronte did not agree.

C. BRONTE: (Waspish) "Her business is not half so much with the human heart, as with the human eyes, mouth, hands and feet."

NARRATOR: Virginia Woolf probably came closest to the truth:

V. WOOLF: "The most perfect artist among women. She is of all great writers, the most difficult to catch in the act of greatness."

1

NARRATOR: Jane, herself, in Northanger Abbey has defined the
              novel.

JANE: "Only a novel. Only a work in which the greatest powers
              of the mind are displayed, in which the most thorough
              knowledge of human nature, the happiest delineation of
              its varieties, the liveliest effusions of wit and humour
              are conveyed to the world in the best chosen language."

                              * * * *

NARRATOR: But in a scene from the same book, Catherine and
              Isabella have quite other ideas."

ISABELLA: Dearest Catherine, what have you been doing with your-
              self all morning? Have you gone on with Udolpho?

CATHERINE: Yes, I have been reading it ever since I woke, and I am
              got to the black veil.

ISABELLA: Are you indeed? How delightful! Oh! I would not tell
              you what is behind the black veil for the world! Are you
              not wild to know?

CATHERINE: Oh! Yes, quite; what can it be? But do not tell me: I
              would not be told upon any account. I know it must be a
              skeleton; I am sure it is Laurentina's skeleton. Oh!
              I am delighted with the book! I should like to spend my
              whole life in reading it, I assure you; if it had not been
              to meet you, I would not have come away from it for all
              the world.

ISABELLA: Dear creature, how much I am obliged to you; and when
              you have finished Udolpho, we will read The Italian
              together; and I have made out a list of ten or twelve
              more of the same kind for you.

CATHERINE: Have you indeed? How glad I am. But are they all
              horrid? Are you sure they are all horrid?

ISABELLA: Yes, quite sure; for a particular friend of mine, one of
              the sweetest creatures in the world, has read every one
              of them. I wish you knew her, you would be delighted
              with her. She is netting herself the sweetest cloak you
              can imagine.

                              * * * *

2

NARRATOR: Fortunately for posterity, Jane only laughed at the
fashion for 'horrid' novels, she did not attempt to
emulate it. If she had, it is unlikely that we should
still be reading her today. About 1870, the time the
verger asked his particular question, the public's
increasing curiosity obliged Jane's nephew, Edward,
then a man in his seventies, to set down in a Memoir
such few facts as he and his two sisters could recall
of their aunt from over half a century before:

EDW. AUSTEN:".. of events her life was singularly barren: few
changes and no great crisis ever broke the smooth
current of its course... I was young when we lost her,
and though I have forgotten much, I have not forgotten
that Aunt Jane was the delight of all her nephews and
nieces. We did not think of her as being clever..
still less as being famous; but we valued her as one
always kind, sympathising and amusing."

NARRATOR: An instance of her special, auntly qualities is evident
in a letter to Caroline, aged ten:

JANE: "I am sorry that you got wet on your ride. Now that
you are become an aunt, you are a person of some consequence and must excite great interest whatever you
do. I have always maintained the importance of aunts
as much as possible, and I am sure of your doing the
same now. Believe me, my dear sister-aunt, yours
affectionately, J. Austen."

NARRATOR: Jane's own father was the Reverend George Austen.
He had married Miss Cassandra Leigh at Bath in
1767, they had then proceeded directly to Steventon
rectory in Hampshire. There they were to spend the
next forty years, and there they were to produce, as
has often been the practice among the poorer English
clergy, a numerous, but remarkable family.

REV. GEORGE
AUSTEN: Steventon, December 17, 1775.

Dear Sister

You have doubtless been for some time in expectation
of hearing from Hampshire, and perhaps wondered a
little we were in our old age grown such bad reckoners,
but so it was, for Cassy certainly expected to have
been

been brought to bed a month ago. However, last night the time came, and without a great deal of warning, everything was soon happily over. We have now another girl, a present plaything for her sister, Cassy, and a future companion. She is to be Jenny. Your sister, thank God, is pure well after it.

Your affectionate brother, George Austen.

NARRATOR: Prophetic words. Jane and Cassandra became, indeed, the most devoted of sisters. In fact, Mrs. Austen once remarked:

MRS. AUSTEN:" If Cassandra were going to have her head cut off, Jane would insist on sharing her fate. "

NARRATOR: Jane. Yes. She was never Jenny, always Jane. Plain Jane Austen, novelist, growing up in an atmosphere more stimulating than was usual in a country parsonage. Her father had been a proctor at Oxford, and he educated in the rectory, several resident students in addition to his own five sons. Elizabeth Bennet, in Pride and Prejudice, was also taught at home, and without any governess, too, as Lady Catherine discovers to her horror:

* * * *

LADY CATHERINE:
Do you play and sing, Miss Bennet?

ELIZABETH: A little

LADY CATHERINE:
Oh! Then some time or other we shall be happy to hear you. Do your sisters play and sing?

ELIZABETH: One of them does.

LADY CATHERINE:
Why did not you all learn? You ought all to have learned. The Miss Webbs all play, and their father has not so good an income as yours. Do you draw?

ELIZABETH: No, not at all.

LADY CATHERINE:
What, none of you?

ELIZABETH: Not one.

LADY CATHERINE:
             That is very strange. Your mother should have taken
             you to town every spring for the benefit of masters.

ELIZABETH: My mother would have had no objection, but my father
             hates London.

LADY CATHERINE:
             Has your governess left you?

ELIZABETH: We never had any governess.

LADY CATHERINE:
             No governess! Five daughters brought up at home
             without a governess! I never heard of such a thing.
             Without a governess, you must have been neglected.

ELIZABETH: Compared with some families, I believe we were;
             but such of us as wished to learn never wanted the
             means. Those who chose to be idle, certainly might.

LADY CATHERINE:
             Aye, no doubt; but that is what a governess will pre-
             vent. And it is wonderful how many families I have
             been the means of supplying in that way, and it was
             but the other day that I recommended another young
             person, who was merely accidentally mentioned to me,
             and the family are quite delighted with her. Mrs.
             Collins, did I tell you of Lady Metcalf's calling yester-
             day to thank me? She finds Miss Pope a treasure.
             'Lady Catherine', said she, 'you have given me a
             treasure.' Are any of your younger sisters out, Miss
             Bennet?

ELIZABETH: Yes, ma'am, all.

LADY CATHERINE:
             All! What, all five out at once? Very odd! And you
             only the second. The younger ones out before the elder
             are married! Your younger sisters must be very young?

ELIZABETH: Yes, my youngest is not sixteen. But really, ma'am,
             I think it would be very hard upon younger sisters,
             that they should not have their share of society and
             amusement, because the elder may not have the
             means or inclination to marry early. The last-born
             has as good a right to the pleasures of youth as the
                                                            first

5

first. And to be kept back on such a motive! I think it would not be very likely to promote sisterly affection or delicacy of mind.

LADY CATHERINE:
Upon my word, you give your opinion very decidedly for so young a person. Pray, what is your age?

ELIZABETH: With three younger sisters grown up, your ladyship can hardly expect me to own it.

NARRATION: Lady Catherine seemed quite astonished at not receiving a direct answer; and Elizabeth suspected herself to be the first creature who had ever dared to trifle with so much dignified impertinence.

* * * *

NARRATOR: Jane was very young when she began to write. She worked in the dressing room that opened off the bedroom she shared with Cassandra. It had a dark chocolate carpet, shelves for books, and Jane's piano. How well one can imagine the peals of laughter coming from behind the door of the little sanctum, as she read aloud to her sister the dedication of her latest work:

JANE:
The History of England
by
a partial, prejudiced and ignorant historian.
To Miss Austen, eldest daughter of the Reverend George Austen, this work is inscribed with all due respect by The Author.

Richard III. The character of this Prince has been in general very severely treated by Historians, but as he was a York, I am rather inclined to suppose him a very respectable man.

Henry VIII. It would be an affront to my Readers were I to suppose that they were not as well acquainted with the particulars of this King's reign as I am myself. It will therefore be saving them the task of reading again what they have read before, and myself the trouble of writing what I do not perfectly recollect, by giving only a slight sketch of the principal Events which marked his reign. The Crimes and Cruelties of this Prince, were too numerous to be mentioned; and nothing can be said in his vindication, but that his abolishing Religious Houses and leaving them to the ruinous

6

ruinous depredations of time has been of infinite
use to the landscape of England in general.

NARRATOR: By the time Jane was seventeen, her five brothers
had all left home. The luckiest one was Edward.
Edward, who was like a boy in a fairy tale, adopted by
Mr. Knight, patron of Steventon, and ultimately inherit-
ing from him two country houses and a large fortune.
Then there were James and Henry. They both went
to Oxford, and while one became a clergyman, the
other started his own bank, issued his own bank notes,
and predictably went bankrupt. Lastly, there were
the sailor brothers, Charles whom Jane called 'our
own particular little brother,' and Frank. They rose
to be admirals. And not merely admirals. Frank
became Admiral of the Fleet, Sir Francis Austen,
K. C. B. , had two wives, seven children, and lived to
be ninety-one.

JANE AUSTEN:
December 28, 1798.

My dear Cassandra

Frank is made. He was yesterday raised to the rank
of commander and appointed to the Peterel sloop, now
at Gibraltar. As soon as you have cried a little for
joy, you may go on and learn further that Lieut. Charles
John Austen is removed to the Tamer frigate, this
comes from the Admiral.

NARRATOR: Jane had a great admiration for the navy. But Sir
Walter Elliot, one of her best drawn characters, has
for the senior service nothing but contempt.

* * * *

JANE: Vanity was the beginning and end of Sir Walter Elliot's
character: vanity of person and of situation. He had
been remarkably handsome in his youth, and at fifty-
four was still a very fine man. Few women could think
more of their personal appearance than he did, or be
more delighted with the place he held in society. He
considered the blessing of beauty as inferior only to
the blessing of a baronetcy; and the Sir Walter Elliot,
who united these gifts, was the constant object of his
warmest respect and devotion.

NARRATOR: Unhappily, however, in spite of these gifts, Sir Walter
has not been able to live within his income, and he now
is faced with the disagreeable necessity of finding a
                                                    tenant

tenant for Kellynch Hall. His agent, Mr. Shepherd,
broaches the subject:

SHEPHERD: I must take leave to observe, Sir Walter, that the
              present juncture is much in our favour. This peace
              will be turning all our rich naval officers ashore.
              Could not be a better time, Sir Walter, for having a
              choice of tenants, very responsible tenants. If a rich
              admiral were to come in our way ...

SIR WALTER: He would be a very lucky man, Shepherd, that's all
              I have to remark. The profession has its utility, but
              I should be sorry to see any friend of mine belonging
              to it.

SHEPHERD: Indeed!

SIR WALTER: Yes; it is in two points offensive to me; first, as being
              the means of bringing persons of obscure birth into
              undue distinction, and, secondly, as it cuts up a man's
              youth and vigour most horribly; a man is in greater
              danger in the navy of being insulted by the rise of one
              whose father his father might have disdained to speak
              to, than in any other line. One day last spring, in
              town, I was in company with two men, striking instances
              of what I am talking of; Lord St. Ives, whose father
              we all know to have been a country curate, without
              bread to eat: I was to give place to Lord St. Ives, and
              a certain Admiral Baldwin, the most deplorable look-
              ing personage you can imagine; his face the colour of
              mahogany, rough and rugged to the last degree; all
              lines and wrinkles, nine grey hairs of a side, and
              nothing but a dab of powder at top. 'In the name of
              heaven, who is that old fellow?' said I to a friend of
              mine who was standing near (Sir Basil Morley).
              'Old fellow!' cried Sir Basil, 'it is Admiral Baldwin.
              What do you take his age to be?' 'Sixty', said I, 'or
              perhaps sixty-two.' 'Forty,' replied Sir Basil, 'forty,
              and no more.' Picture to yourselves my amazement:
              I shall not easily forget Admiral Baldwin. I never
              saw quite so wretched an example of what a seafaring
              life can do; but to a degree. They are all knocked
              about, and exposed to every climate, and every weather,
              till they are not fit to be seen. It is a pity they are
              not knocked on the head at once, before they reach
              Admiral Baldwin's age.

                              * * * *

NARRATOR: The navy was at the height of its glory in Jane's
              lifetime. It was the era of Nelson and Villeneuve, of
              Trafalgar and St. Domingo. Many ships Jane refers
                                                               to

8

to in her novels are those in which Frank had actually
served. She must have met many of his brother
officers, and indeed, Jane was as fond of flirtation,
fine clothes and a ball as any of her own heroines.
And these innocent pleasures are often the subject of
her youthful correspondence, a fact which her critics
have seized upon in order to accuse her of triviality.

JANE: "Eliza has seen Lord Craven at Barton. She found his
manners very pleasing indeed. The little flaw of
having a Mistress now living with him at Ashdown Park,
seems to be the only unpleasing circumstance about him. "

"Mrs. Hall, of Sherborne, was brought to bed yesterday of a dead child, some weeks before she expected,
owing to a fright. I suppose she happened unawares
to look at her husband. "

NARRATOR: Jane little dreamed when she imparted this piece of
gossip to amuse her sister, that it would pursue her
into posterity. Indeed, it is to Cassandra, who paid
every year a long visit to their rich brother, Edward
Knight, at Godmersham Park in Kent, that most of the
surviving letters are written. Surviving, because
Cassandra admitted to having destroyed all the most
significant and revealing correspondence after Jane died.

JANE: To Miss Austen, Godmersham Park, Kent

My dear Cassandra

I took the liberty a few days ago of asking your black
velvet Bonnet to lend me its cawl, which it very
readily did, and by which I have been enabled to give a
considerable improvement of dignity to my cap, which
was too nidgetty to please me, and instead of the black
military feather shall put in the coquelicot one, as
being smarter; and besides Coquelicot is to be all the
fashion this winter. People get so horribly poor and
economical in this part of the world, I have no patience
with them. Kent is the only place for happiness.
Everybody is rich there.

NARRATOR: If Edward was a prince in a fairy tale, whenever either
Jane or Cassandra stayed at Godmersham, they must
have felt like Cinderella at the palace. French wines
and ices, Jane writes of, and that she is sitting in a
room with five tables, eight and twenty chairs and two
fires all to herself. A contrast, indeed, from the
humble parlour and homemade orange wine at the

Austen's

Austen's. In fact, it would appear that there was about as much discrepancy between Edward's style of living and that of the Austen's, as there was between the two branches of the Dashwood family in <u>Sense and Sensibility.</u>

* * * *

NARRATION:Mrs. John Dashwood did not at all approve of what her husband intended to do for his sisters. To take three thousand pounds from the fortune of their dear little boy, would be impoverishing him to the most dreadful degree. She begged him to think again on the subject. How could he answer it to himself to rob his child, and his only child too, of so large a sum? And what possible claim could the Miss Dashwoods, who were related to him only by half blood, which she considered as no relationship at all, have on his generosity to so large an amount?

Mr.DASHWOOD:
It was my father's last request to me, that I should assist his widow and daughters.

Mrs. DASHWOOD:
He did not know what he was talking of, I dare say: ten to one but he was lightheaded at the time. Had he been in his right senses, he could not have thought of such a thing as begging you to give away half your fortune from your own child.

Mr. DASHWOOD:
He did not stipulate for any particular sum, my dear Fanny: he only requested me, in general terms, to assist them, and make their situation more comfortable than it was in his power to do. Perhaps it would have been as well if he had left it wholly to myself. He could hardly suppose I should neglect them. But as he required the promise, I could not do less than give it: at least I thought so at the time. Something therefore must be done for them.

Mrs.DASHWOOD:
Well, then, <u>let</u> something be done for them; but <u>that</u> something need not be three thousand pounds. Consider, that when the money is once parted with, it never can return.

Mr. DASHWOOD:
> Why, to be sure. The time may come when Harry will
> regret that so large a sum was parted with. Perhaps,
> then, it would be better for all parties if the sum were
> diminished one half, it would be a prodigious increase
> to their fortunes.

Mrs. DASHWOOD:
> Oh, beyond anything great! What brother on earth
> would do half as much for his sisters, even if really
> his sisters! And as it is - only half blood! But you
> have such a generous spirit!

Mr. DASHWOOD:
> I would not wish to do anything mean, one had rather,
> on such occasions, do too much than too little. No
> one, at least, can think I have not done enough for them:
> they can hardly expect more.

Mrs. DASHWOOD:
> There is no knowing what they may expect, but we
> are not to think of their expectations: the question is,
> what you can afford to do.

Mr. DASHWOOD:
> Certainly, and I think I may afford to give them five
> hundred pounds apiece. As it is, without any addition
> of mine, they will each have about three thousand pounds
> on their mother's death: a very comfortable fortune
> for any young woman.

Mrs. DASHWOOD:
> To be sure it is: and, indeed, it strikes me that they
> can want no addition at all. If they marry, they will
> be sure of doing well; and if they do not, they may all
> live very comfortably together.

Mr. DASHWOOD:
> That is very true, and, therefore, I do not know
> whether, upon the whole, it would not be more advisable
> to do something for their mother while she lives rather
> than for them; something of the annuity kind, I mean.
> A hundred a year would make them all perfectly com-
> fortable.

Mrs. DASHWOOD:
> To be sure, it is better than parting with fifteen hun-
> dred pounds at once. But then, if Mrs. Dashwood should
> live fifteen years, we shall be completely taken in.

Mr. DASHWOOD:
      Fifteen years! My dear Fanny; her life cannot be
worth half that purchase.

Mrs. DASHWOOD:
      Certainly not; but if you observe, people always live
for ever when there is any annuity to be paid them; and
she is very stout and healthy, and hardly forty. An
annuity is a very serious business; it comes over and
over every year, and there is no getting rid of it. I
have known a great deal of the trouble of annuities;
for my mother was clogged with the payment of three
to old superannuated servants by my father's will, and
it is amazing how disagreeable she found it. Twice
every year, these annuities were to be paid, and then
there was the trouble of getting it to them; and then one
of them was said to have died, and afterwards it turned
out to be no such thing. My mother was quite sick of it.

Mr. DASHWOOD:
      It is certainly an unpleasant thing to have those kind of
yearly drains on one's income. To be tied down to the
regular payment of such a sum is by no means desirable;
it takes away one's independence.

Mrs. DASHWOOD:
      Undoubtedly: and, after all, you have no thanks for it.
They think themselves secure and it raises no gratitude
at all. If I were you, whatever I did should be done at
my own discretion entirely. It may be very inconven-
ient some years to spare a hundred, or even fifty
pounds, from our own expenses.

Mr. DASHWOOD:
      I believe you are right, my love; it will be better
that there should be no annuity in the case; whatever
I may give them occasionally will be of far greater
assistance than a yearly allowance. Because they
would only enlarge their style of living if they felt sure
of a larger income and would not be a sixpence the
richer for it at the end of the year. A present of fifty
pounds, now and then, will prevent their ever being
distressed for money, and will, I think, be amply dis-
charging my promise to my father.

Mrs. DASHWOOD:
      To be sure it will. Indeed, to say the truth, I am con-
vinced that your father had no idea of your giving
them any money at all. The assistance he thought of,
I dare say, was only such as looking out for a comfortable small house for them, helping them to move
                             their

their things, and sending them presents of fish and
game, whenever they are in season. I'll lay my
life that he meant nothing further. Altogether, they
will have five hundred a year amongst them, and what
on earth can four women want for more than that?
They will live so cheap! Their housekeeping will be
nothing at all. They will have no carriage, no horses,
and hardly any servants; they will keep no company,
and can have no expenses of any kind! Five hundred
a year! I am sure I cannot imagine how they will spend
half of it; and as to your giving them more, it is quite
absurd to think of it. They will be much more able
to give you something.

* * * *

NARRATOR: Could it be a coincidence that five hundred pounds was
exactly the sum that Mrs. Austen and her daughters
had to live on after Mr. Austen died? But this is to
anticipate. At the time Jane was contriving her cap
and adding poppy-coloured feathers, Mr. Austen was
still alive and rector of Steventon. It was in the dressing
room, at the age of twenty, that she sat down to begin
her most famous work, First Impressions, later re-
titled, Pride and Prejudice.

JANE AUSTEN: June 11, 1799

My dear Cassandra
I would not let Martha read First Impressions again
upon any account, and am very glad that I did not leave
it in your power. She is very cunning, but I saw
through her design; she means to publish it from
memory, and one more perusal must enable her to do it.

NARRATOR: Two years earlier, when the manuscript was first
completed, Jane's father had sent it up to London.
But Mr. Cadell, publisher of Sir Walter Scott, would
not touch Jane Austen, and thus he lost the opportunity
of bringing out a novel which has since been trans-
lated into twenty-five languages, and which contains
many immortal characters, including that most
spirited of all heroines, Elizabeth Bennet:

* * * *

NARRATION: Elizabeth had been obliged, by the scarcity of gentlemen, to sit down for two dances; and during part of
that time, Mr. Darcy had been standing near enough
for her to overhear a conversation between him and
Mr. Bingley, who came from the dance for a few
minutes, to press his friend to join it.

BINGLEY: Come, Darcy, I must have you dance. I hate to see you standing about by yourself in this stupid manner. You had much better dance.

DARCY: I certainly shall not. You know how I detest it, unless I am particularly acquainted with my partner. At such an assembly as this it would be insupportable. Your sisters are engaged, and there is not another woman in the room whom it would not be a punishment to me to stand up with.

BINGLEY: I would not be so fastidious as you are, for a kingdom! Upon my honour, I never met so many pleasant girls in my life as I have this evening; and there are several of them you see uncommonly pretty.

DARCY: You are dancing with the only handsome girl in the room,

NARRATION: Said Mr. Darcy, looking at the eldest Miss Bennet.

BINGLEY: Oh! She is the most beautiful creature I ever beheld! But there is one of her sisters sitting down just behind you, who is very pretty, and I dare say very agreeable. Do let me ask my partner to introduce you.

DARCY: Which do you mean?

NARRATION: And turning round he looked for a moment at Elizabeth, till catching her eye, he withdrew his own and coldly said:

DARCY: She is tolerable, but not handsome enough to tempt me; I am in no humour at present to give consequence to young ladies who are slighted by other men. You had better return to your partner and enjoy her smiles, for you are wasting your time with me.

NARRATION: Mr. Bingley followed his advice. Mr. Darcy walked off; and Elizabeth remained with no very cordial feelings toward him. She told the story, however, with great spirit among her friends; for she had a lively playful disposition, which delighted in anything ridiculous.

* * * *

NARRATOR: A criticism by Jane's detractors, is that she has only one plot...the husband hunt. How did she, herself, fare at this interesting sport?
One of her admirers was Tom Lefroy, who later became Chief Justice of Ireland. Jane was twenty when she met Tom. He was staying with his aunt, Mrs. Lefroy at Ashe:

JANE AUSTEN: My dear Cassandra

In the first place I hope you will live twenty-three years longer. Mr. Tom Lefroy's birthday was yesterday, so that you are very near of an age. You scold me so much in the nice long letter which I have this moment received from you, that I am almost afraid to tell you how my Irish friend and I behaved. Imagine to yourself everything most profligate and shocking in the way of dancing and sitting down together. He is a very gentlemanlike, good-looking, pleasant young man, I assure you. He is so excessively laughed at about me at Ashe, that he is ashamed of coming to Steventon, and ran away when we called on Mrs. Lefroy a few days ago.....
after I had written the above, we received a visit from Mr. Tom Lefroy and his cousin. He has but one fault..it is that his morning coat is a great deal too light.

I look forward with great impatience to our party to Ashe tomorrow night, as I rather expect to receive an offer from my friend in the course of the evening. I shall refuse him, however, unless he promises to give away his white coat.

NARRATOR: Tom Lefroy did not make an offer. He was poor and needed to marry well. But when he was a very old man he confessed that as a boy he had been in love with Jane Austen.
But is this cause for regret?
It was soon after he left the neighborhood that Jane began First Impressions. Supposing she had married him? Supposing she had become the wife of the Chief Justice of Ireland and the mother of a family?
(PAUSE)
What in the world would have happened to Elizabeth Bennet and Darcy?

* * * *

SIR WILLIAM LUCAS:
(A 'common' accent)
>You must allow me, Mr. Darcy, to present this
young lady to you as a very desirable partner. You
cannot refuse to dance, I am sure, when so much
beauty is before you.

NARRATION:
>And taking Elizabeth's hand, Sir William would have
given it to Mr. Darcy who, though extremely surprised, was not unwilling to receive it, when she
instantly drew back, and said with some discomposure.

ELIZABETH:
>Indeed, sir, I have not the least intention of dancing.
I intreat you not to suppose that I moved this way
in order to beg for a partner.

NARRATION:
>Mr. Darcy, with grave propriety, requested to be
allowed the honour of her hand, but in vain.
Elizabeth was determined; nor did Sir William at
all shake her purpose by his attempt at persuasion.

SIR WILLIAM:
>You excel so much in the dance, Miss Eliza, that
it is cruel to deny me the happiness of seeing you;
and though this gentleman dislikes the amusement
in general, he can have no objection, I am sure, to
oblige us for one half hour.

ELIZABETH:
>(Smiling) Mr. Darcy is all politeness.

SIR WILLIAM:
>He is indeed; but considering the inducement, my
dear Miss Eliza, we cannot wonder at his complai-
sance - for who would object to such a partner?

NARRATION:
>Elizabeth looked archly, and turned away. Her
resistance had not injured her with the gentleman,
and he was thinking of her with some complacency,
when thus accosted by Miss Bingley:

MISS BINGLEY: I can guess the subject of your reverie.

DARCY: I should imagine not.

MISS BINGLEY: You are considering how insupportable it would be to
pass many evenings in this manner - in such society;
and indeed I am quite of your opinion. I was never

more

16

more annoyed! The insipidity, and yet the noise - the nothingness, and yet the self-importance of all those people! What would I give to hear your strictures on them,

DARCY: Your conjecture is totally wrong, I assure you. My mind was much more agreeably engaged. I have been meditating on the very great pleasure which a pair of fine eyes in the face of a pretty woman can bestow.

NARRATION: Miss Bingley immediately fixed her eyes on his face, and desired he would tell her what lady had the credit of inspiring such reflections. Mr. Darcy replied with great intrepidity:

DARCY: Miss Elizabeth Bennet.

MISS BINGLEY: Miss Elizabeth Bennet! I am all astonishment. How long has she been such a favourite? And pray, when am I to wish you joy?

DARCY: That is exactly the question which I expected you to ask. A lady's imagination is very rapid; it jumps from admiration to love, from love to matrimony, in a moment. I knew you would be wishing me joy.

MISS BINGLEY: Nay, if you are serious about it, I shall consider the matter is absolutely settled. You will have a charming mother-in-law, indeed; and, of course, she will be always at Pemberley with you.

NARRATION: He listened to her with perfect indifference while she chose to entertain herself in this manner; and as his composure convinced her that all was safe, her wit flowed long.

* * * * * * *

INTERVAL

Act 11

NARRATOR: The Regency must have been a pleasant period in
which to live. (PAUSE) That is, if you were a man.
A woman could not work, could not travel, could
not leave the house alone. And when she married,
her money and possessions became the property of
her husband, and every year it was her inevitable
duty to bear a child.

JANE: "Mrs. Tilson's remembrance gratifies me; but poor
woman! How can she be honestly breeding again."

"Good Mrs. Deedes! I hope she will get the better
of this, and then I would recommend to her and
Mr. Deedes, the simple regimen of separate bedrooms."

NARRATOR: Jane's sisters-in-law had an unfortunate propensity
for dying in childbirth. Nor did rank exempt one
from this danger. Queen Charlotte, wife of George
the Third, had fifteen children, and her granddaughter,
Princess Charlotte, only child of the Prince Regent and
in her generation sole legitimate heir to the throne,
died at her first confinement, aged twenty-one. Jane
wrote to her favourite niece, Fanny, daughter of her
rich brother, Edward Knight:

JANE: "Depend upon it, the right man will come at last, and
by not beginning the business of mothering quite so
early in life, you will be young in constitution, spirits,
figure and countenance, while Mrs. William Hammond
is growing old by confinements and nursing."

NARRATOR: Jane had another niece, Anna, a girl greatly gifted in
drawing and writing, who had now renounced these
pursuits to marry a poor country clergyman and begin
on a monotonous career of annual reproduction:

JANE: "Anna has not a chance of escape; her husband called
here the other day and said she was pretty well, but
not equal to so long a walk. Poor Animal, she will
be worn out before she is thirty. I am very sorry for

                                                      her

18

her. Mrs. Clement, too, is in that way again. I am quite tired of so many children. Mrs. Benn has a thirteenth."

NARRATOR: But was there any alternative? In <u>Pride and Prejudice</u> Charlotte Lucas has the answer:

CHARLOTTE: Her reflections were in general satisfactory. He, to be sure, was neither sensible nor agreeable; but still he would be her husband. Without thinking highly either of men or of matrimony, marriage had always been her object; it was the only honourable provision for well-educated young women of small fortune, and however uncertain of giving happiness, must be their pleasantest preservative from want

NARRATOR: It is this fact which spurs on Mrs. Bennet to find husbands for her five daughters, because when Mr. Bennet dies, Mr. Collins will inherit his estate.

* * * *

NARRATION: On finding Mrs. Bennet, Elizabeth, and one of the younger girls together, soon after breakfast, Mr. Collins addressed the mother in these words:

MR. COLLINS: May I hope, madam, for your interest with your fair daughter Elizabeth, when I solicit for the honour of a private audience with her in the course of this morning?

NARRATION: Before Elizabeth had time for anything but a blush of surprise, Mrs. Bennet instantly answered:

MRS. BENNET: Oh dear! Yes--certainly. I am sure Lizzy will be very happy - I am sure she can have no objection. Come, Kitty, I want you upstairs.

ELIZABETH: Dear madam, do not go. I beg you will not go. Mr. Collins can have nothing to say to me that anybody need not hear. I am going away myself.

MRS. BENNET: No, no, nonsense, Lizzy. I desire you will stay where you are. Lizzy, I <u>insist</u> upon your staying and hearing Mr. Collins.

19

NARRATION: A moment's consideration making Elizabeth sensible that it would be wisest to get it over with as soon as possible; she sat down again.

MR. COLLINS: Believe me, my dear Miss Elizabeth, that your modesty, so far from doing you any disservice, rather adds to your other perfections. You would have been less amiable in my eyes had there not been this little unwillingness; but allow me to assure you, that I have your respected mother's permission for this address. But before I am run away with my feelings on the subject, perhaps it would be advisable for me to state my reasons for marrying.

NARRATION: The idea of Mr. Collins, with all his solemn composure, being run away with by his feelings, made Elizabeth so near laughing, that she could not use the short pause he allowed in any attempt to stop him farther, and he continued:

MR. COLLINS: First, that I think it a right thing for every clergyman to set the example of matrimony in his parish; secondly, that I am convinced it will add very greatly to my happiness; and thirdly - that it is the particular advice and recommendations of the very noble lady whom I have the honour of calling patroness.

Allow me, by the way, to observe, my fair cousin, that you will find Lady Catherine's manners beyond anything I can describe; and your wit and vivacity, I think, must be acceptable to her, especially when tempered with the silence and respect which her rank will inevitably excite. But the fact is that being as I am, to inherit this estate after the death of your honoured father (who, however, may live many years longer), I could not satisfy myself without resolving to choose a wife from among his daughters, that the loss to them might be as little as possible, when the melancholy event takes place.
Now nothing remains for me but to assure you in the most animated language of the violence of my affection.

ELIZABETH: You are too hasty, sir. I am very sensible of the honour of your proposals, but it is impossible for me to do otherwise than decline them.

MR. COLLINS: It is usual with young ladies to reject the addresses of the man whom they secretly mean to accept. I am therefore by no means discouraged by what you have just said, and shall hope to lead you to the altar ere long.

ELIZABETH: Upon my word, sir, your hope is rather an extra-
ordinary one after my declaration. You could not
make me happy, and I am convinced I am the last
woman in the world who could make you so Nay,
were your friend Lady Catherine to know me, I am
persuaded she would find me in every respect ill
qualified for the situation.

MR. COLLINS: Were it certain that Lady Catherine would think so.
(He hesitates), but I cannot imagine that her ladyship
would at all disapprove of you. And you may be certain
that when I have the honour of seeing her again, I
shall speak in the highest terms of your modesty,
economy, and other amiable qualifications.

ELIZABETH: Indeed, Mr. Collins, all praise of me will be unneces-
sary. In making me the offer, you must have satisfied
the delicacy of your feelings with regard to my family,
and may take possession of Longbourn estate whenever it falls, without any self-reproach.

NARRATION: Mr. Collins was not left long to the silent contempla-
tion of his successful love, for Mrs. Bennet, having
dawdled about in the vestibule to watch for the end of
the conference, no sooner saw Elizabeth open the door,
and with a quick step pass her towards the staircase,
then she entered the breakfast room. Mr. Collins
then proceeded to relate the particulars of their inter-
view, with the result of which he trusted he had every
reason to be satisfied. Mrs. Bennet would have been
glad to be equally satisfied, but she dared not believe
it, and could not help saying so.

MRS. BENNET: But depend upon it, Mr. Collins, that Lizzy shall be
brought to reason. She is a very headstrong, foolish
girl, and does not know her own interest; but I will
make her know it.

MR. COLLINS: Pardon me for interrupting you, madam, but if she
is really headstrong and foolish, perhaps it would be
better not to force her into accepting me, because if
liable to such defects of temper, she could not contri
bute much to my felicity.

MRS. BENNET: Sir, you quite misunderstand me.. Lizzy is only headstrong in such matters as these. In everything else
she is as good-natured a girl as ever lived. I will go
directly to Mr. Bennet, and we shall very soon settle
it with her, I am sure.

NARRATION: She would not give him time to reply, but hurrying
             instantly to her husband, called out as she entered
             the library:

MRS.BENNET: Oh, Mr. Bennet, you are wanted immediately; we
             are all in an uproar. You must come and make
             Lizzy marry Mr. Collins, for she vows she will not
             have him, and if you do not make haste he will change
             his mind and not have <u>her.</u>

NARRATION: Mr. Bennet raised his eyes from his book as she
             entered, and fixed them on her face with a calm uncon-
             cern which was not in the least altered by her communi-
             cation.

MR. BENNET: I have not the pleasure of understanding you. Of what
             are you talking?

MRS.BENNET: Of Mr. Collins and Lizzy. Lizzy declares she will
             not have Mr. Collins, and Mr. Collins begins to say
             that he will not have Lizzy.

MR. BENNET: And what am I to do on the occasion?

MRS.BENNET: Speak to Lizzy about it yourself. Tell her that you
             insist upon her marrying him.

MR. BENNET: Let her be called down. She shall hear my opinion.

NARRATION: Mrs. Bennet rang the bell, and Miss Elizabeth was
             summoned to the library.

MR. BENNET: Come here, child. I have sent for you on an affair
             of importance. I understand that Mr. Collins has
             made you an offer of marriage. Is it true?

ELIZABETH: Yes, sir.

MR. BENNET: Very well, and this offer of marriage you have
             refused?

ELIZABETH: I have, sir.

MR. BENNET: Very well. We now come to the point. Your mother insists upon your accepting it.

MRS. BENNET: Yes, or I will never see her again.

MR. BENNET: An unhappy alternative is before you, Elizabeth. From this day you must be a stranger to one of your parents. Your mother will never see you again if you do not marry Mr. Collins, and I will never see you again if you do.

* * * *

NARRATOR: But however satirically Jane depicts the marriage game in her novels, her views in real life were rather different. Some of her most revealing letters are to her favourite niece, Fanny Knight:

JANE: "And now, my dear Fanny, having written so much on one side of the question, I shall turn around and entreat you not to commit yourself further, and not to think of accepting him unless you really do like him. Anything is to be preferred or endured rather than marrying without affection; and if his deficiencies of manner strike you more than all his good qualities, give him up at once. Your trying to incite your own feelings by a visit to his room amused me excessively. The dirty shaving rag was exquisite. Such a circumstance ought to be in print. Much too good to be lost. "

NARRATOR: Tantalizing glimpses are all we have of Jane's one serious love affair. She and Cassandra were staying at a resort in the west of England. There Jane met a man whom even Cassandra later recalled has having such charm of person, mind and manner, as to make him fully worthy of her sister. They fell in love, parted, planning to meet again, but shortly afterwards news came of his sudden death.

That was the end of any thoughts of marriage for Jane. Her books were her children, and though she was not yet aware of it, the time was coming when she would send them out into the world, because something happened at Godmersham that affected them all. The previous ten years had been neither happy nor prosperous ones for Jane. Mr. Austen had died, and the widow and daughters had shifted about as best they might in various lodgings in a variety of places. Then Edward's wife died following the birth of her eleventh child and Edward at last came forward and offered his mother and sisters a home. The house decided on was in the village

village of Chawton, in their old county of Hampshire.

JANE: "There are six bedchambers at Chawton; Henry wrote to **my** mother the other day and luckily mentioned the number, which is just what we wanted to be assured of. He speaks also of Garrets for store-places, one of which she immediately planned fitting up for Edward's Manservant, and now perhaps it must be for our own, for she is already quite reconciled to our keeping one. The difficulty of doing without had been thought of before. His name shall be Robert, if you please."

NARRATOR: Chawton suited Jane. Here she found the peace of mind to begin three new novels and to revise the three she had already written. Here she found the courage to commission the publishing of her own work. It was in 1811 when Jane was thirty-six years old that the first of her novels appeared:

Jane writes to Cassandra:

JANE: "No, indeed, I am never too busy to think of Sense and Sensibility. I can no more forget it than a mother can forget her sucking child; and I am much obliged to you for your enquiries.

NARRATOR: Only fourteen months later Pride and Prejudice came into the world.

JANE: "I feel that I must write to you today. I want to tell you that I have got my own darling child from London. Miss Benn dined with us on the very day of the book's coming, and in the evening we fairly set at it, and read half the first volume to her, prefacing that, having intelligence from Henry that such a work would soon appear, we had desired him to send it whenever it came out, and I believe it passed with her unsuspected. She was amused, poor soul!.. she really does seem to admire Elizabeth. I must confess that I think her as delightful a creature as ever appeared in print."

* * * *

If a shorter script is desired, the next scene may be omitted, proceeding directly to * page 29.

24

NARRATION: At five o'clock Miss Bingley and Mrs. Hurst retired
to dress, and at half past six Elizabeth was summoned
to dinner. To the civil enquiries which then poured
in, she could not make a very favourable answer.
Jane was by no means better. When dinner was over,
she returned directly to her sister, and Miss Bingley
began abusing her as soon as she was out of the room.
Her manners were pronounced to be very bad indeed,
a mixture of pride and impertinence; she had no conversation, no stile, no taste, no beauty. Mrs. Hurst
thought the same, and added,

MRS. HURST: She has nothing, in short, to recommend her, but
being an excellent walker. I shall never forget her
appearance this morning. She really looked almost
wild.

MISS BINGLEY:
She did indeed, Louisa, I could hardly keep my countenance. Very nonsensical to come at all! Why must
she be scampering about the country, because her sister
had a cold?

MRS. HURST: Yes, and her petticoat; I hope you saw her petticoat,
six inches deep in mud, I am absolutely certain; and
the gown which had been let down to hide it, not doing
its office.

BINGLEY: Your picture may be very exact, Louisa,

NARRATION: said Mr. Bingley.

BINGLEY: but this was all lost upon me. I thought Miss Elizabeth
Bennet looked remarkably well. Her dirty petticoat
quite escaped my notice.

MISS BINGLEY:
You observed it, Mr. Darcy, I am sure. And I am
inclined to think that you would not wish to see your
sister make such an exhibition.

DARCY: Certainly not.

MISS BINGLEY:
To walk three miles, or four miles, or five miles, or
whatever it is, above her ancles in dirt, and alone,
quite

quite alone! What could she mean by it? It seems to me to shew an abominable sort of conceited independence, a most country town indifference to decorum.

BINGLEY: It shews an affection for her sister that is very pleasing.

MISS BINGLEY:
                I am afraid, Mr. Darcy, that this adventure has rather affected your admiration of her fine eyes.

DARCY: Not at all. They were brightened by the exercise.

NARRATION: A short pause followed this speech, and Mrs. Hurst began again.

MRS. HURST: I have an excessive regard for Jane Bennet, she is really a very sweet girl, and I wish with all my heart she were well settled. But with such a father and mother, and such low connections, I am afraid there is no chance of it.

DARCY: I think I have heard you say, that their uncle is an attorney in Meryton.

MRS. HURST: Yes; and they have another, who lives somewhere near Cheapside.

MISS BINGLEY:
                That is capital. (The two ladies laugh heartily)

BINGLEY: If they had uncles enough to fill all Cheapside, it would not make them one jot less agreeable.

DARCY: But it must very materially lessen their chance of marrying men of any consideration in the world.

NARRATION: To this speech Bingley made no answer; but his sisters indulged their mirth for some time at the expense of their dear friend's vulgar relations. With a renewal of tenderness, however, they repaired to her room on leaving the dining-parlour, and sat with her till summoned to coffee. Elizabeth would not quit Jane

                                                        till

26

till late in the evening, when she had the comfort of
seeing her asleep, and when it appeared to her rather right
than pleasant that she should go downstairs herself.
On entering the drawing-room she found the whole
party at loo. She drew near the cardtable and stationed
herself to observe the game.

MISS BINGLEY:
Is Miss Darcy much grown since the spring?

NARRATION: Inquired Miss Bingley.

MISS BINGLEY:
Will she be as tall as I am?

DARCY: I think she will. She is now about Miss Elizabeth
                Bennet's height, or rather taller.

MISS BINGLEY:
How I long to see her again! I never met with anybody
who delighted me so much. Such a countenance, such
manners! And so extremely accomplished for her age!
Her performance on the piano-forte is exquisite.

BINGLEY: It is amazing to me, how young ladies can have
                patience to be so very accomplished, as they all are.

MISS BINGLEY:
All young ladies accomplished! My dear Charles, what
do you mean?

BINGLEY: Yes, all of them, I think. They all paint tables, cover
                skreens and net purses. I scarcely know anyone who
                cannot do all this, and I am sure I never heard a young
                lady spoken of for the first time, without being infor-
                med that she was very accomplished.

DARCY: Your list has too much truth. The word is applied to
                many a woman who deserves it no otherwise than by
                netting a purse, or covering a skreen. I am very far
                from agreeing with you in your estimation of ladies
                in general. I cannot boast of knowing more than half
                a dozen in the whole range of my acquaintance, that
                are really accomplished.

27

MISS BINGLEY:
>Nor, I, I am sure.

ELIZABETH: Then you must comprehend a great deal in your idea
of an accomplished woman.

NARRATION: observed Elizabeth.

DARCY: Yes, I do comprehend a great deal.

MISS BINGLEY:
>Oh! certainly, no one can be really esteemed accom-
plished who does not have a thorough knowledge of
music, singing, drawing, dancing, and the modern
languages to deserve the word; and besides all this,
she must possess a certain something in her air and
manner of walking, the tone of her voice, her address
and expressions, or the word will be but half deserved.

DARCY: All this she must possess, and to all this she must
yet add something more substantial, in the improvement
of her mind by extensive reading.

ELIZABETH: I am no longer surprised at your knowing only six
accomplished women. I rather wonder now at your
knowing any.

DARCY: Are you so severe upon your own sex, as to doubt the
possibility of all this.

ELIZABETH: "I never saw such a woman. I never saw such capacity,
and taste, and application, and elegance, as you describe, united.

NARRATION: Mrs. Hurst and Miss Bingley both cried out against
the injustice of her implied doubt, and were both
protesting that they knew many women who answered
this description, when Mr. Hurst called them to order,
with bitter complaints of their inattention to what was
going forward. As all conversation was thereby at an
end, Elizabeth soon afterwards left the room.

MISS BINGLEY:
>Eliza Bennet,

NARRATION: said Miss Bingley, when the door was closed on her,

MISS BINGLEY:
               is one of those young ladies who seek to recommend
               themselves to the other sex, by undervaluing their own;
               and with many men, I dare say, it succeeds. But, in
               my opinion, it is a paltry device, a very mean art.

DARCY: Undoubtedly,

NARRATION: replied Mr. Darcy, to whom this remark was chiefly
               addressed,

DARCY: there is meanness in all the arts which ladies some-
               times condescend to employ for captivation. Whatever
               bears affinity to cunning is despicable.

NARRATION: Miss Bingley was not so entirely satisfied with this
               reply as to continue the subject.

                              * * * *

NARRATOR: * Jane's nephew, Edward, has told us under what con-
               ditions she worked at Chawton.

EDWARD AUSTEN:
               "She had no separate study to retire to and most of the
               work must have been done in the general sitting-room,
               subject to all kinds of casual interruptions. She was
               careful that her occupation should not be suspected by
               servants, or visitors, or any persons beyond her own
               family party. She wrote upon small sheets of paper
               which could easily be put away, or covered with a piece
               of blotting paper. There was, between the front door
               and the offices, a swing door which creaked when it
               was opened; but she objected to having this little incon-
               venience remedied, because it gave her notice when
               anyone was coming."

NARRATOR: This insistence of Jane's on anonymity was interesting.
               She had a genuine dislike of publicity. None of her
               novels appeared under her name in her lifetime. Her
               immediate family was sworn to silence, and except
               for Fanny, not even her own nieces and nephews were
               let in on the secret. Then her brother, Henry, hearing
               a titled lady praise Pride and Prejudice could not
               resist boasting that it was the work of his sister, and
                                                            so

29

so her authorship became common knowledge. Edward, a schoolboy of fourteen at Winchester in his excitement and pride, burst forth into verse:

BOY: To Miss J. Austen

No words can express, my dear Aunt, my surprise
Or make you conceive how I opened my eyes,
Like a pig Butcher Pile has just struck with his knife,
When I heard for the very first time in my life.
That I had the honour to have a relation
Whose works were dispersed through the whole of
                                    the Nation.
I assure you, however, I'm terribly glad;
Oh dear! Just to think (and the thought drives me mad)
That you (not young Ferrars) found out that a ball
May be given in cottages, never so small.
And though Mr. Collins, so grateful for all,
Will Lady de Bourgh his dear Patroness call,
'Tis to your ingenuity really he owed
His living, his wife, and his humble abode.

NARRATOR: Inspired by their aunt's success, Edward and his two
             sisters also began to write. They showered her with
             manuscripts for her consideration, and found her never
             too tired or too busy to respond:

             To Caroline, aged ten:

JANE: "I wish I could finish stories as fast as you can..the
             good for nothing father should not escape unpunished.
             I hope he hung himself or took the surname of Bone,
             or underwent some direful penance or other."

NARRATOR: To Anna, aged twenty-one:

JANE: "You are now collecting your people delightfully, getting
             them exactly into such a spot as is the delight of my
             life. Three or four families in a country village is the
             very thing to work on; and I hope you will write a great
             deal more, and make full use of them while they are so
             very favourably arranged."

NARRATOR: To Edward, aged eighteen:

JANE: "My dear Edward. I am quite concerned for the loss
             your mother mentions in her letter. Two chapters and
             a half to be missing is monstrous! It is well that I have
             not been at Steventon lately, and therefore cannot be
             suspected of purloining them; two strong twigs and a
                                                            half

30

half towards a nest of my own would have been something. I do not think, however, that any theft of that
sort would be really very useful to me. What should
I do with your strong, manly vigorous sketches, full
of variety and glow? How could I possibly join them on
to the little bit (two inches wide) of ivory on which I
work with so fine a brush, as produces little effect
after much labour?"

NARRATOR: As her books came out, no longer at her own expense,
              and as her name became known, so did her fame in-
              crease, even into royal circles. Notice came from no
              less a personage than the Prince Regent himself. Now
              Jane was no admirer of the Prince Regent, nor of the
              way he treated his wife:

JANE: "Poor woman, I shall support her as long as I can,
              because she is a woman, and because I hate her husband. "

NARRATOR: Jane may have hated the prince; but the prince adored
              Jane. He kept a set of her books in each of his country
              houses, and hearing that she was staying in London
              with her brother Henry, he asked his librarian, the
              Reverend James Stanier Clarke, to give her permission
              to dedicate any future work to him.

              Jane, disconcerted, writes to Mr. Clarke:

JANE: "Sir: I intreat you to have the goodness to inform me
              how such a permission is to be understood and whether
              it is incumbent on me to show my sense of the honour. "

NARRATOR: Mr. Clarke answers in some surprise:

REV. J. S. CLARKE:
              "Dear Madam:
              It is certainly not incumbent on you to dedicate your
              work now in the press to His Royal Highness; but if
              you wish to do the Regent that honour either now or at
              any future period, I am happy to send you that permis-
              sion, which need not require any more trouble or
              solicitation on your part. "

NARRATOR: Nor was this the end of the correspondence.
              Mr. Clarke continued to shower Jane with advice,
              encouragement and a host of suggestions:

J. S. CLARKE: Pray continue to write. Do let us have an English clergyman after your fancy, shew dear Madam what good would be done if Thythes were taken away entirely, and describe him burying his own mother, as I did. I have never recovered from the shock.

NARRATOR: The Prince Regent now appointed Mr. Clarke secretary and chaplain to young Prince Leopold of Saxe Coburg, who was in England awaiting his forthcoming marriage to Princess Charlotte. The marriage that was to end with her death in childbirth.

Mr. Clarke writes again to Jane:

J. S. CLARKE: Perhaps when you again appear in print you may choose to dedicate your volumes to Prince Leopold. Any historical romance, illustrative of the history of the august House of Cobourg, would just now be very interesting.

> Believe me at all times,
> dear Miss Austen
> Your obliged friend   J. S. Clarke"

NARRATOR: This was too much for Jane.

JANE: "I could no more write a romance than an epic poem. I could not sit seriously down to write a serious romance under any other motive than to save my life; and if it were indispensable for me to keep it up and never relax into laughing at myself or other people, I am sure I should be hung before I had finished the first chapter.

NARRATOR: But fortunately, as Virginia Woolf said, Jane wrote "not for the Prince Regent or his librarian, but for the world at large." Emma, the very novel which she eventually did dedicate to His Royal Highness contains some of her most comic characters. One of them is Mrs. Elton who has come to call on Emma, at Hartfield:
                              * * * *

NARRATION: The very first subject, after being seated, was Maple Grove.

MRS. ELTON: My brother, Mr. Suckling's, seat;

NARRATION: A comparison of Hartfield to Maple Grove. Mrs. Elton
             seemed most favourably impressed by the size of the
             room, the entrance, and all that she could see or imagine.

MRS. ELTON: Very like Maple Grove indeed! I'm quite struck by
             the likeness. That room is the very shape and size of
             the morning-room at Maple Grove. And the staircase.
             You know, as I came in, I observed how very like the
             staircase was; placed exactly in the same part of the
             house. I really could not help exclaiming! I assure
             you, Miss Woodhouse, it is very delightful to me to be
             reminded of a place I am so extremely partial to as
             Maple Grove.

NARRATION: Emma made as slight a reply as she could; but it was
             fully sufficient for Mrs. Elton, who only wanted to be
             talking herself.

MRS. ELTON: So extremely like Maple Grove! And it is not merely
             the house; the grounds, I assure you, as far as I could
             observe, are strikingly like. The laurels at Maple
             Grove are in the same profusion as here, and stand
             very much in the same way --just across the lawn;
             and I had a glimpse of a fine large tree, with a bench
             round it, which put me so exactly in mind! My
             brother and sister will be enchanted with this place.
             People who have extensive grounds themselves are
             always pleased with anything in the same style.

NARRATION: Emma doubted the truth of this sentiment. She had a
             great idea that people who had extensive grounds
             themselves cared very little for the extensive grounds
             of anybody else; but it was not worthwhile to attack
             an error so double-dyed.

MRS. ELTON: My brother and sister have promised us a visit in the
             spring, or summer at farthest, and that will be our
             great time for exploring. While they are with us we
             shall explore a great deal, I dare say. They will have
             their barouche-landau, of course, which holds four
             perfectly; and therefore, without saying anything of
             our carriage, we should be able to explore the different
             beauties extremely well. They would hardly come in
             their chaise, I think, at that season of the year. Indeed,
             when the time draws on, I shall decidedly recommend
             their bringing the barouche-landau; it would be so
             very much preferable. When people come into a
             beautiful country of this sort, you know, Miss Woodhouse,
             one naturally wishes them to see as much as possible;
             and Mr. Suckling is extremely fond of exploring. We
                                                        explored

explored to King's-Weston twice last summer, in
that way, most delightfully, just after their first
having the barouche-landau. You have many parties
of that kind here, I suppose, Miss Woodhouse, every
summer ?

* * * *

NARRATOR: Also in Emma, and at the opposite pole from Mrs.
Elton, is simple, lovable, boring Miss Bates, a fascina-
ting example of how Jane could take an acquaintance
from real life and create a character. For there seems
little doubt that some friends of the Austens who lived
near Godmersham are the originals of Mrs. and Miss
Bates.

JANE: "We had our dinner party on Wednesday with the
addition of Mrs. and Miss Milles. Both mother and
daughter are much as I have always found them. I like
the mother because she is cheerful and grateful for
what she is at the age of ninety and upwards..
Miss Milles was queer as usual, and provided us with
plenty to laugh at. She undertook in three words to
give us the history of Mrs. Scudamore's reconciliation,
and then talked on about it for half an hour, using such
odd expressions, and so foolishly minute, that I could
hardly keep my countenance. "

NARRATOR: Having met Miss Milles, let us compare Miss Bates,
herself, as she accompanies her niece, Jane Fairfax,
to the supper room at the ball:

* * * *

MISS BATES: Jane, Jane, my dear Jane, where are you? - Here is
your tippet. Mrs. Weston begs you to put on your
tippet. She says she is afraid there will be draughts
in the passage, though everything has been done. One
door nailed up. Quantities of matting. My dear Jane,
indeed you must. Yes, my dear, I ran home, as I
said I should, to help grandmamma to bed, and got
back again, and nobody missed me. I set off without
saying a word, just as I told you. Grandmamma was
quite well, had a charming evening with Mr. Woodhouse,
biscuits, and baked apples and wine before she came
away: and she inquired a great deal about you, how
you were amused, and who were your partners. 'Oh!'
said I, 'I shall not forestall Jane; I left her dancing
with Mr. George Otway; she will love to tell you all
about it herself tomorrow: her first partner was
Mr. Elton, I do not know who will ask her next, perhaps Mr. William Cox.' My dear sir, you are too
obliging. Is there nobody you would not rather? I am
not

34

not helpless. Sir, you are most kind. Upon my word,
Jane on one arm, and me on the other! Well, here we
are at the passage. Two steps, Jane, take care of
the two steps. Oh! no, there is but one. Well, I was
persuaded there were two. How very odd! I was convinced there were two, and there is but one. I never
saw anything equal to the comfort and style. Candles
everywhere. I was telling you of your grandmamma,
Jane, - there was a little disappointment. The baked
apples and biscuits, excellent in their way, you know;
but there was a delicate fricassee of sweetbread and
some asparagus brought in at first, and good Mr.
Woodhouse, not thinking the asparagus quite boiled
enough, sent it all out again. Now there is nothing grandmamma loves better than sweetbread and asparagus -
so she was rather disappointed, but we agreed we would
not speak of it to anybody, for fear of its getting round
to dear Miss Woodhouse, who would be so very much
concerned! - Well, this is brilliant! I am all amaze-
ment! could not have supposed anything! Such elegance
and profusion! I have seen nothing like it since - Well,
where shall we sit? Anywhere, so that Jane is not in
a draught. Where I sit is of no consequence. Oh! do
you recommend this side? - Well, I am sure, - only it
seems too good - but just as you please. Dear Jane,
how shall we ever recollect half the dishes for grandmamma?

* * * *

NARRATOR: This is the kind of fine brush work on the little piece
of ivory that brought Jane money - pewter, she called
it, and recognition. She went more often to stay with
Henry in Sloane Street. Henry was at this time a banker,
and successful man of affairs in London. While she
was in town, Jane helped Edward, a widower with eleven
children, to choose a dinner service at Wedgewood's,
and accompanied him when he took his daughters to the
dentist.

JANE: "The poor girls and their teeth! I have not mentioned
them yet, but we were a whole hour at Spence's, and
Lizzy's were filed and lamented over again and poor
Marianne had two taken out after all, the two just beyond the eye teeth, to make room for those in front.
When her doom was fixed, Fanny, Lizzy and I walked
into the next room, where we heard each of the two
sharp hasty screams. I would not have had him look
at mine for a shilling a tooth and double it. It was a
disagreeable hour. "

NARRATOR: In such homely ways as these, did Jane share in the
domestic life of her brothers. And it was probably on

one

35

one of them that she modelled that most endearing of
married couples, Admiral and Mrs. Croft. For
Mrs. Croft cannot endure to be parted from her hus-
not even when he goes to sea.

MRS. MUSGROVE:
What a great traveller you must have been, ma'am!

NARRATION: said Mrs. Musgrove to Mrs. Croft.

MRS. CROFT: Pretty well, ma'am, in the fifteen years of my marriage;
though many women have done more. I have crossed
the Atlantic four times, and have been once to the
East Indies and back again, and only once; beside being
in different places about home; But I never went beyond the Streights, and never was in the West Indies.
We do not call Bermuda or Bahama, you know, the
West Indies.

NARRATION: Mrs. Musgrove had not a word to say in dissent; she
could not accuse herself of having ever called them
anything in the whole course of her life.

MRS. CROFT: And I do assure you, ma'am, that nothing can exceed
the accommodations of a man-of-war; and I can safely
say that the happiest part of my life has been spent
on board a ship. The only time that I ever really
suffered in body or mind, the only time that I ever
fancied myself unwell, or had any ideas of danger, was
the winter that I passed by myself at Deal, when the
Admiral (Captain Croft then) was in the North Seas.
I lived in perpetual fright at that time, and had all
manner of imaginary complaints from not knowing what
to do with myself, or when I should hear from him
next; but as long as we could be together, nothing ever
ailed me, and I never met with the smallest incon-
venience.

* * * *

NARRATOR: It is Charles who seems to have been the most likely
brother to have furnished the example for the Crofts,
because his wife and three little girls all lived with
him on board the Namur. This did not suit the eldest,
little Cassy, aged five, and there had been some talk
of her coming to live with her grandmother and aunts
at Chawton. Jane was staying with Edward Knight at
Godmersham when Charles and his family arrived for
a visit.

36

JANE: "They came last night about seven. They had a very
rough passage, he would not have ventured if he had
known how bad it would be. They are both looking very
well, but poor little Cassy is grown extremely thin
and looks poorly. I talk to her about Chawton; she
remembers much but does not volunteer on the subject.
Poor little love. Papa and Mama have not yet made
up their mind as to parting with her or not. The chief,
indeed the only difficulty with Mama is a very reason-
able one, the child's being very unwilling to leave
them. At the same time, she has been suffering so
much lately from sea sickness, that her Mama cannot
bear to have her much on board this winter. I do not
know how it will end, or what is to determine it."

NARRATOR: What finally determined it was the usual tragedy as a
result of which Cassy came frequently to stay at
Chawton. The next year, on board the Namur, Charles's
wife gave birth to her fourth child, and neither she nor
the baby survived the ordeal.

As sympathetic aunt, as valued sister and as successful
author, these too few happy, prosperous years flew by.
Her nieces and nephews were growing up. Edward
Austen had just finished Winchester:

JANE: My dear Edward

One reason for my writing to you now, is that I may have
the pleasure of directing to you Esquire. I give you joy
of having left Winchester. Now you may own, how miser-
able you were there; now, it will gradually all come out,
your crimes and your miseries how often you went up by
the mail to London and threw away fifty guineas at a
tavern, and how often you were on the point of hanging
yourself, restrained only as some ill-natured aspersion
upon poor old Winchester has it, by want of a tree within some miles of the city.

NARRATOR: A few months before she wrote this letter, Jane had
finished what was to be her last completed work,
Persuasion was given its title by Henry, and published
after her death. Many people have identified her with
the heroine, Anne Elliot; the most famous of whom is
Kipling. Yet Persuasion is not, like her first novel,
'light and bright and sparkling.' It has more of humanity
and compassion than her other books, and in telling the
story of Anne Elliot's enduring love, perhaps Jane is
speaking for herself. In the final scene, Capt. Wentworth,
who had some years earlier been engaged to Anne, is writing
a letter, while in another part of the same room Anne
tries

tries to convince his friend, Captain Harville that
woman's love is more constant than man's.

* * * *

ANNE ELLIOT:
        Your feelings may be strongest.

NARRATION: Replied Anne to Captain Harville.

ANNE ELLIOT:
        But women's are the most tender. Man is more robust
than woman, but he is not longer-lived. You are always
labouring and toiling, exposed to every risk and hard-
ship. Your home, country, friends, all quitted. Neither
time, nor health nor life, to be called your own. It
would be too hard indeed (with a faltering voice) if woman's
feelings were to be added to all this.

HARVILLE: We shall never agree upon this question.

NARRATION: Captain Harville was beginning to say, when a slight
               noise called their attention to Captain Wentworth's
               hitherto perfectly quiet division of the room. It was
               nothing more than that his pen had fallen down, but
               Anne was startled at finding him nearer than she had
               supposed, and half inclined to suspect that the pen had
               only fallen, because he had been occupied by them,
               striving to catch sounds, which yet she did not think
               he could have caught.

HARVILLE: (Lowered voice) Well, Miss Elliot, as I was saying
               we shall never agree, I suppose, upon this point.

ANNE ELLIOT:
        Men have had every advantage of us in telling their own
story.

HARVILLE: But how shall we prove anything?

ANNE ELLIOT:
        We never shall.

HARVILLE: Ah! If I could but make you comprehend what a man suffers when he takes a last look at his wife and children, and watched the boat that he has sent them off in, as long as it is in sight, and then turns away and says, 'God knows whether we ever meet again!'

And then, if I could convey to you the glow of his soul when he does see them again. If I could explain to you all this, and all that a man can bear and do, and glories to do, for the sake of these treasures of his existence! I speak, you know, only of such men as have hearts.

ANNE: Oh, I hope to do justice to all that is felt by you, and by those who resemble you. God forbid that I should under-value the warm and faithful feelings of any of my fellow creatures. No, I believe you capable of everything great and good in your married lives. So long as -- if I may be allowed the expression, so long as you have an object. I mean while the woman you love lives, and lives for you. All the privilege I claim for my own sex (it is not a very enviable one; you need not covet it) is that of loving longest, when existence or when hope is gone!

WENTWORTH: ... I can listen no longer in silence. ... I must speak to you... by such means as are within my reach.... dare not say..that man forgets sooner than woman, that his love has an earlier death...for you alone, I think and plan. Have you not seen this? ..I had not waited could I have read your feelings...I can hardly write, I am every instant hearing something which overpowers me. Too good. Too excellent creature. You do us justice, indeed. You do believe there is true attachment and constancy among men. Believe it to be most fervent, most undeviating in ... Frederick Wentworth.

NARRATOR: Fifteen years old to forty. For so long Jane had laboured at her craft, and now, now when she had achieved success, confidence, recognition, now when she had everything to live for, her health began to fail.

Her nephew, Edward, wrote in his Memoir:

EDW. AUSTEN: "I cannot tell how soon she was aware of the serious nature of her malady. By God's mercy it was not attended by much suffering; so that she was able to tell her friends..and perhaps to persuade herself that, excepting want of strength, she was 'otherwise very well.'"

39

NARRATOR: By the spring of 1817, her symptoms could no longer
             be ignored. She and Cassandra removed to lodgings
             at Winchester, in order that she might be under the
             care of Mr. Lyford, a noted surgeon. One of her last
             letters, her beautiful handwriting sadly deteriorated,
             is to Edward, now at Oxford:

JANE: There is no better way, my dearest Edward, of thank-
             ing you for your affectionate concern for me during my
             illness than by telling you myself, as soon as possible,
             that I continue to get better. I will not boast of my hand-
             writing; neither that nor my face have yet recovered
             their proper beauty, but in other respects I gain strength
             very fast. Mr. Lyford says he will cure me, and if he
             fails I shall draw up a memorial and lay it before the
             Dean and Chapter, and have no doubt of redress from
             that pious, learned and disinterested body. Our lodg-
             ings are very comfortable. We have a neat little draw-
             ing room with a bow window overlooking Dr. Gabell's
             garden. God bless you, my dear Edward. If ever you
             are ill, may you be as tenderly nursed as I have been.
             May the same blessed alleviations of anxious, sym-
             pathising friends be yours: and may you possess, as I
             dare say you will, the greatest blessing of all in the
             consciousness of not being unworthy of their love.
             I could not feel this.

                        Your   very affectionate aunt,

                                Jane Austen

                            * * * * * *

Appendix

For the assistance of the director and actors not intimately acquainted with the novels of Jane Austen, there follows a description of some of the characters in Jane Austen's own words.

Catherine and Isabella Make Friends at Bath

CATHERINE MORLAND

"her heart was affectionate, her disposition cheerful and open, without conceit or affectation of any kind, her manners just removed from the awkwardness and shyness of a girl; her person pleasing, and, when in good looks, pretty - and her mind about as ignorant and uninformed as the female mind at seventeen usually is."

ISABELLA THORPE

"being four years older than Miss Morland, and at least four years better informed.. could rectify the opinions of her new friend in many articles of tasteful attire; could discover a flirtation between any gentleman and lady who only smiled on each other; and point out a quiz through the thickness of a crowd."

From: Pride and Prejudice

ELIZABETH BENNET

"Mr. Darcy had at first scarcely allowed Elizabeth to be pretty; he had looked at her without admiration at the ball; and when they next met, he looked at her only to criticise. But no sooner had he made it clear to himself and his friends that she had hardly a good feature in her face, than he began to find it was rendered uncommonly intelligent by the beautiful expression of her dark eyes. To this discovery succeeded some other equally mortifying. He was forced to acknowledge her figure to be light and pleasing; and in spite of his asserting that her manners were not those of the fashionable world, he was caught by their easy playfulness."

DARCY

"Mr. Darcy soon drew the attention of the room by his fine, tall, person, handsome features, noble mien; and the report which was in general circulation within five minutes after his entrance, of his having ten thousand a year. The gentlemen pronounced him to be a fine figure of a man, and the ladies declared he was much handsomer than Mr. Bingley, and he was looked at with great admiration for about half the evening, till his manners gave a disgust which turned the tide of his popularity; for he was discovered to be proud, to be above his company, and above being pleased; and not all his large estate in Derbyshire could then save him from having a most forbidding, disagreeable countenance, and being unworthy to be compared with his friend."

42

BINGLEY

"he is just what a young man ought to be, sensible, good humoured, lively; and I never saw such happy manners! So much ease, with such perfect good breeding!"

MISS BINGLEY AND MRS. HURST

She and her sister "were very fine ladies, not deficient in good humour when they were pleased, nor in the power of being agreeable where they chose it; but proud and conceited. They were rather handsome, had been educated in one of the first seminaries in town, had a fortune of twenty thousand pounds, were in the habit of associating with people of rank; and were therefore in every respect entitled to think well of themselves, and meanly of others."

MR. COLLINS

"Mr. Collins was not a sensible man, and the deficiency of nature had been but little assisted by education or society; the greatest part of his life having been spent under the guidance of an illiterate and miserly father. The subjection in which his father had brought him up, had given him originally great humility of manner, but it was now a good deal counteracted by the self-conceit of a weak head, living in retirement, and the consequential feelings of early and unexpected prosperity. A fortunate chance had recommended him to Lady Catherine de Bourgh; and the respect which he felt for her high rank, and his veneration for her as his patroness, mingling with a very good opinion of himself, of his authority as a clergyman, and his rights as a rector, made him altogether a mixture of pride and obsequiousness, self-importance and humility."

LADY CATHERINE

"Lady Catherine was a tall, large woman, with strongly marked features, which might once have been handsome. Her air was not conciliating, nor was her manner of receiving them, such as to make her visitors forget their inferior rank. She was not rendered formidable by silence; but whatever she said, was spoken in so authoritative a tone, as marked her self-importance."

SIR WILLIAM LUCAS

"had been formerly in trade in Meryton, where he had made a tolerable fortune and risen to the honour of knighthood by an address to the King, during his mayoralty. The distinction had perhaps been felt too strongly. It had given him a disgust to his business and to his residence in a small market town; and quitting
them

them both, he had removed with his family to .. where he could
think with pleasure of his own importance, and unshackled by
business occupy himself solely in being civil to all the world.
For though elated by his rank, it did not render him supercilious;
on the contrary, he was all attention to everybody. By nature
inoffensive, friendly and obliging, his presentation at St. James's
had made him courteous."

MR. AND MRS. BENNET

"Mr. Bennet was so odd a mixture of quick parts, sarcastic humour,
reserve, and caprice, that the experience of three and twenty years
had been insufficient to make his wife understand his character.
Her mind was less difficult to develop. She was a woman of mean
understanding, little information, and uncertain temper. When she
was discontented she fancied herself nervous. The business of her
life was to get her daughters married; its solace was visiting and
news."

From: Emma

MRS. ELTON

"self-important, presuming, familiar, ignorant, and ill-bred.
She had a little beauty and a little accomplishment, but so little
judgement that she thought herself coming with superior knowledge of the world, to enliven and improve a country neighborhood."

MISS BATES

"Miss Bates enjoyed a most uncommon degree of popularity for a
woman neither young, handsome, rich, nor married. She had no
intellectual superiority to make atonement to herself, or frighten
those who might hate her, into outward respect. She had never
boasted either beauty or cleverness. Her youth had passed without distinction, and her middle of life was devoted to the care of a
failing mother, and the endeavour to make a small income go as
far as possible. And yet she was a happy woman, and a woman
whom no one named without good-will. It was her own universal
good-will and contented temper which worked such wonders. She
loved everybody, was interested in everybody's happiness, quick-
sighted to everybody's merits. She thought herself a most fortunate
creature, and surrounded with blessings in such an excellent mother
and so many good neighbours and friends. The simplicity and
cheerfulness of her nature, her contented and grateful spirit, were
a recommendation to everybody and a mine of felicity to herself.
She was a great talker on little matters .... "

A Few Years Before Persuasion Opens:

Capt. Wentworth, at that time, a remarkably fine young man, with a great deal of intelligence, spirit and brilliancy; and Anne an extremely pretty girl, with gentleness, modesty, taste and feeling. Half the sum of attraction on either side, might have been enough, for he had nothing to do, and she had hardly anybody to love, but the encounter of such lavish recommendations could not fail. They were gradually acquainted, and when acquainted, rapidly and deeply in love.

A short period of exquisite felicity followed, and but a short one. Troubles soon arose. Sir Walter..on being applied to for his consent, gave it all the negative of great astonishment, great coldness, great silence, and a professed resolution of doing nothing for his daughter. He thought it a very degrading alliance.

Anne Elliot, with all her claims of birth, beauty and mind, to throw herself away at nineteen; involve herself in an engagement with a young man, who had nothing but himself to recommend him.. in the chances of a most uncertain profession, and no connexions to secure even his farther rise in that profession....

Anne, young and gentle as she was, was persuaded to believe the engagement a wrong thing, indiscreet, improper, hardly capable of success, and not deserving it. But it was not merely a selfish caution, under which she acted.. she imagined she was consulting his good, even more than her own..He left the country in conse-quence.

As Persuasion Opens

ANNE ELLIOT

"Anne, with an elegance of mind and sweetness of character, which must have placed her high with any people of real understanding, was nobody with either father or sister; her word had no weight; her convenience was always to give way; she was only Anne. A few years before, Anne Elliot had been a very pretty girl, but her bloom had vanished early."

CAPT. WENTWORTH

The years which had destroyed her (Anne Elliot's) youth and bloom had only given him a more glowing, manly, open look, in no respect lessening his personal advantages.
.." a certain glance of his bright eye, and curl of his handsome mouth, "..
.." but one opinion of Capt. Wentworth..It was unvarying, warm admiration everywhere."

45